FUR COATS IN TAHITI

Jeremy Over was born in Leeds in 1961. His poetry was first published in *New Poetries II*. There followed two Carcanet collections, *A Little Bit of Bread and No Cheese* and *Deceiving Wild Creatures*. He currently lives on a hill near Llanidloes in the middle of Wales.

*Jeremy Over*

# FUR COATS IN TAHITI

CARCANET

First published in Great Britain in 2019 by
Carcanet
Alliance House, 30 Cross Street
Manchester M2 7AQ
www.carcanet.co.uk

A CIP catalogue record for this book is
available from the British Library.
ISBN 978 1 78410 763 5

Book design by Andrew Latimer
Printed in Great Britain by SRP Ltd, Exeter, Devon

The publisher acknowledges financial
assistance from Arts Council England.

*For Marita and in memory of my mother*

# CONTENTS

# FUR COATS IN TAHITI

O

A wistful nocturne is cycling
idly across the ceiling
by the rose and the cup of water;
the rose, the against whom rose is
whistling O Magnum Mysterium.

et ad-mi - ra - - bi - le,  et ad - - mi-ra-bi-le sa - cra-men -tum
et ad-mi - ra - - bi - le,  et ad - - mi-ra-bi-le sa - cra-men -tum
et ad-mi - ra - - bi - le,  et ad - - mi-ra-bi-le sa - cra-men -tum
et ad-mi - ra - - bi - le,  et ad - - mi-ra-bi-le sa - cra-men -tum

The lemons are an Easter fruit and the Virgin
is a dissonant appoggiatura G-sharp from the altos; a bum note
that, with the oranges in blossom, indicates renewed life.
Beata Virgo stands out against a consonant backdrop
with great care on the polished surface of the table.

Blessed is the Virgin who at five in the morning,
at the umpteenth stroke of midnight
cycles across the ceiling towards a crack
of light between the door and the night and the day
that animals ut a-ni - ma - - li - a
should see the new-born Lord
lying in a manger.

                    Al - le - lu - - ia! Al - le - lu - - ia!

            Al-le-lu - ia!                   Al - le - lu - - ia!

    Al - le - lu - - ia!              Al - le - lu - - ia!

            Al - le - lu - - ia!          Al - le - lu - - ia!

## ANY FOOL

can count the seeds in an apple but
what emerges most forcefully from Edwin Mullin's
handsomely illustrated book which might never
have come to public notice if it hadn't been for the efforts
of, on the one side, the harbour and on the other, anything
he could lay his hands on climbing into the basket
of a hot air balloon but that's not the best way the best
way to predict the future is to invent it
and the best way to remember the past is to invent it
and the best way to live in the present is less carefully
one way's in a jar with a tiny wooden spoon or in a hat
my granny wouldn't have been seen dead in a Chinese landscape:
craggy mountains, bamboo houses, rivers, weeping willow trees – the lot
then a necklace of green black and finally a sea shell yes
finally a joss stick but any fool can count the apples in a tree or a seed
and any fool can count on God on the fingers of one hand

CUMBERLAND

Summers in the mountains and tundra
are short

And so some summers the fist unfolds
and some summers not

In Cumberland the fist unfolds in bracken fronds and foxgloves
illumination pink

## THE TINKLING CHARM OF GOLDFINCHES

has just hoisted a Schoenhut
upright toy piano

to our first floor
bathroom window

using a system of pulleys
and winches

## ASH

It seems to hang lifelessly now in midsummer leaf
but here comes the wind
moving through the fields of barley
like a pack of hounds on the trail of a day

when the same tree was loud with an anxiety
of winter thrushes which, as I approached,
made it breathe in and then just let go,
giving everything up; the full deck of cards spread out across the sky.

## H.C. KIND MAN

The years pass simply: blue, white, yellow.
Feet become mushrooms
often intractably
and an apparent banality circles around my thoughts
completely moving the shoes
to Vienna
said Vienna
the city mourns in the violet clumps.

It is again a merry again and again
out: shedding mountain encyclopaedias
somewhat left of my suspect bicycle
or snow on hot bread waking
with an inclination for the punchline solemn
and pleasing for the other whoms behind the sofa
wherein Dandytum the son of a shoemaker
rules out all the larger travellers
with a strong interest in smearing.

Nut marks foam in the garden
when the early cock is to meet the day
like a red tongue that cock cries red
it is a red tongue and the tongue
snaps out at the roof
snaps out at the root
and the eyes open again and again and we couple the horses and cattle
down in the damp green clover for sweet slow juice lurking
all somewhat shower-romantic
in the highest tree tops' open latches
and with it the first lark's
squatting gush
as nature shows up time and again
and is met with hostility.

In the blossom with reading glasses. The idea of sitting in the blossom, amongst the plum trees. The idea of the bees and a glass of beer. The idea of 'no ideas'. The idea of 'things'. The septic tank, the curve of the road and the idea of traffic. The farmer and his ideas. Amazed sheep with big vertical lift off ears. Sheep and the idea of big ears and amazement. Bees buzzing. The sounds of ideas buzzing above my head. The idea of my head. And passing crows. The idea passing overhead of passing overhead. Counting plum trees and the ideas of counting. Plum trees and crows passing overhead. And the shit lying soft in the septic tank.

Bringing me beer, the idea of that. And my sun hat, midges, beard. Walt Whitman dropping in with a few words. No ideas exactly, just a few things to add. Dandelions and blossom on the floor. The idea of the orchard floor. The ground beneath us and gorse in the distance. The idea of distance and yellow. Trousers in the shade, the idea of shade, the idea of 'in the'. The idea in the trousers.

Fungus in the grass. The idea of spreading. A robin's song. Deckchairs on the move. William Carlos Williams coming to sit in the orchard. The idea of 'the' and 'my'. Hark at him. At the idea of harking. The idea of his/her orchard. *The Orchard Upstairs*. Penelope's idea. Up the ladder to the idea of *The Orchard Upstairs*. The house casting a shadow. 17.43. Half way across the lawn. The idea of the lawn cast across the lawn.

The idea repeating itself. The idea of the thing repeating. The pleasure of the idea of spaghetti though the world may be ending is ending the idea of ending is ending in endless repeats across the lawn in triplicate the idea of ending in triplicate and anchovies. The idea of anchovy sauce and mackerel and spaghetti, the curve of the road in duplicate. The endless complaint of sheep. The unsatisfactory nature of life right here and now. The idea of that. And what did you expect exactly? Bees humming certainly. The idea of humming certainly. Amazement. The expectation of amazement. And beyond the idea of expectation, the comfort of moss beneath the feet. Feet in the idea of moss the idea of that. Das ding in sich. Yes. Lesser Celandine. But. Lesser than what?

The idea of
primrose being
thrown at the bank

Geworfenheit

# MOUNTAINS AND RIVERS
*After Tommy Cooper*

spoon jar
jar spoon
spoon jar jar
spoon jar jar
spoon spoon jar jar
spoon jar spoon jar
jar spoon spoon
spoon jar spoon glass

bottle bottle glass
spoon jar glass bottle
glass jar bottle glass
bottle jar spoon bottle
jar bottle jar spoon spoon bottle glass egg
spoon jar jar spoon

## SHE

*'Having happily had it with a spoon'*
— Gertrude Stein, *'Four Saints in Three Acts'*

Had never been married.
Had not loved her in the way she had intended so to do.
Had lovely eyes.
Had asked her to look after her canary.
Had said, can't you come home with us, we have to have some
Americans in our house.
Had already arrived at the station.
Had earrings like a gypsy and a father who is the King of Poland.
Had done all the publicity.
Had been hiding under a false name.
Had the paws and muzzle shaved.
Had no money.
Had no plans for the summer or winter.
Had only planted potatoes.
Had overheard a woman saying it in French in a restaurant.
Had tried 'Fletcherism'.
Had seen its prototype in the Cluny Museum.
Had previously written prose of such convoluted strangeness, that
few people knew what she was talking about.
Had the courage to tell them to go to hell.
Had the place wired for electricity.
Had the pioneer's passion for buying useless real estate.
Had never seen a plane up close before and was unsure how people
got in them.
Had problems with the traffic.
Had to step over the concierge.
Had to part.
Had something to do with cows.

Had their teeth filled and went to the Grand Canyon.
Had become a rubber merchant.
Had been, was now no more.
Had had it.
Had it with a spoon.

LOVE LETTERS

Something stands in for each day of Lent
like a birthday, no ups and downs
but love on love and plenty of cushions
pushed into the hollow of each
and the punt pole anchors between
the bed and the china door knobs.

Stand in the rain for as long as you can
to sense the passionate life of Christ
and the spread out self – a long spray of iris
turns up its collar, while around the corner
was another 'me'… the collapsing
green in a nest of red tipped up to form
an easel I've had to, and still have to, stand by,
where I remember willows and sunlight.

She was talking through the wall
and meaning, in her loveliness, scolloped leaves.
The remarkable thing is what they make coffee in
or tip it out of. The little cups of what there is not.

And so they are, as it were, at home.
There is a white hedge of May and some Cow Parsley
wallpaper. The picture shows nothing
is so peaceful as privacy in a lavatory.

Reading from left to right
her hand disappears into a tree
and meaning, in her loveliness,
all the pages of a book, an open book.

# THE FINE ART OF WRITING
*After Ernst Jandl*

in poetry, to say it one more time, we need all that to which we have
not become accustomed; we need it to begin poetry at all, and we need
it to make even the very first steps towards understanding poetry,
something which is itself a beginning. Everything to which we have
not become something; we need it to begin something at all, and we need
in something, to say something one more time, we need all that to which
we have not become fully something so long as, with every something, a new
something begins for us. I believe we will all of us come to the end of our somethings
without even something of us having become something, and we have a word
for this something of the utmost something which is itself something.
Something to which something something with every something, a new
something somethings for us. Everything to something not something
to itself. We need something no longer to begin something at all.
We just need to say something one more time. Something.

# EAT YOUR CHERRIES MARY

*For Steve Reich and Dan Maskell*

> *'O eat your cherries, Mary*
> *O eat your cherries now*
> *O eat your cherries Mary*
> *That grow upon the bough'*
> — *The Cherry Tree Carol*

O eat your cherries Mary
O eat your cherries now
O eat your cherries Mary
O eat your cherries now
O eat your cherries
O eat your cherries
O each or cherries
O each or cherries O
each or cherries O
eat your cherries O
eat your cherries O
each or cherries O
each or each or
reach or each or
reach o'er reach
your reach o'er reach
your reach or each
or each of each
of each or

of each or

of each or

slivovic or

slivovic or

Zivojinovic

Slobodan
Zivojinovic

eat your cherries
Slobodan

## THE FULL ENGLISH BREAKFAST

Containing what Rudolf downhill lemons
crabapple parquet flooring psychopathology
Mont Blanc                    blancmange
the feathered highlights of blancmange
a body of work picked up downhill
picked up in the streets downhill
this much picked up at least
downhill the chewed hat
chewed hat with attitude

You can see the hunter's heart. He's in the act of peeing. You can see his penis. An airplane flies across the sky while a fisherman fishes from a boat. There is also a big tree, a carob tree; on one side there is a rifle, and on the other, a fish. Everything happens at the same time. The fisherman fishes while the airplane is flying overhead and the hunter is peeing the first letters of the word *sardine*. All that makes up a story.

The lake is empty.
It is waiting for fish.

The field keeps very still.
It is waiting for celandine.

It feels the need to work more freely, more gaily – to 'proliferate'.

I feel in great shape.
Here is the eye.
There is the nose
and there is the moustache.

Look at the nose: the nostrils are shaped like testicles.

It doesn't matter.

The organ music and the light filtering through the stained glass windows to the interior gloom suggest forms to me in the wandering eucharist of dried saliva, hard sponges and hair clippings from which luminous waterfalls come shooting out while the herons of the Old and New Testaments are set in clockwork motion and begin their dance.

# ARTIFICIALLY ARRANGED SCENES

*After the films of George Méliès*

Whatever one wants in his world
is what it seems: legs, arms,
an undulating seductress
UT UT RE SI UT
whatever.

Takes off his own head six times
and throws them onto telegraph wires
where they remain familiar with the sea
in an elegant second empire drawing room.

The wolf being somewhat tied and shut up
in a collection of prolonged standing-on-legs scenes,
while the chorus in pink satin cutaway coats
boil the old lady in her own scullery copper not even
                                        trapdoors thought of,
creeps behind falling snow.

Lanterns dissolve and disembark from a pleasure boat.
Treads on hose. A veritable sledgehammer chez Robert.
And men into women leads to another mysterious box.
Christ, in pumps, on water, takes a Madeleine Bastille omnibus
but before long becomes tired of the Salvation Army and women
forced into prostitution by the tropical conditions only yards from his body.

Likewise a real goat eating hay in 1832
separates the Davenport Brothers
takes the bags of gold and uses bellows
to inflate his own vigorous rendition of the, then popular, cake walk

as a funnel, also in reverse, a wing
ending in the valley of Chamonix
chugs through an obviously fake mountain scene
bearing the glass slippers in their cabinet.

# FIRE

Are you prepared to take part in discontinuous strike action? She waves her hands, shifts her gaze, gestures briefly. We're in Bob's room. The quirky triangular face. On a little old train and so on. Turning the film itself into a box which I would call a distraction. When we get there, a solar or lunar eclipse is paired with the image of an object falling into a circular pool of water. Sitting here I can move my lips as though I were talking. Something I really liked and wanted to be with like a chair or jar of pâté. The belief that, on a daily basis, living things arise from non-living material. Sound is an aesthetic error. Aphids arise from the dew on plants projected through a deep blue filter to impart the same hue universally used in the silent era to signify night. She dreams that my aunt had laid a coal fire and got it published before a match had even been struck. The very moment sound is removed my theory is that it becomes more possible to see 'swan-necked' flasks and an end to the debate over spontaneous generation.

## TURNING HOGS INTO THE WOODS

In glandage, the season of turning hogs into the woods,
I impart, I pronounce, I communicate as tidings
I deliver, bestow and utter
I also use in the manufacture of glass
You, on the other hand, bear acorns or other nuts and you (pl.) allude
While he or she shoots or darts a ray of light or splendour
And we all fly off in an oblique direction
And they twinkle

## MY FORTHCOMING TOMETTE

feminine noun

     hexagonal floor tile     or     single portion ready to eat French meal (Made in New Zealand) In 2 minutes on your plate

Example Sentences:

Un seul motif, mais trois coloris: safran, tomette et olivier.
MARIE CLAIRE

Trends:

Used rarely. 'tomette' is in the lower 50% of commonly used words in the dictionary.

Our Graph of Recorded Usage shows that from 1898 to 1932 there was a big slump in the use of 'tomette', followed by a jagged period when it was apparently either used everyday (on everyone's lips as it were) until 1972 when it fell off the scale where it has lain on the floor only occasionally climbing up to be spoken again.

Nearby:

tombola
Tombouctou
tome
tomette
tomographie
tomographie par emission de positions
ton

Things to do in Timbuktu:

| | | |
|---|---|---|
| breadcrumbing | *Aug 28 2017* | *dropping hints to someone that you are interested in them romantically with no intention of following through* |
| stashing | *Aug 28 2017* | *starting a relationship with someone but not making it public in any way* |

Pending:

| | | |
|---|---|---|
| implinth | *Aug 28 2017* | *to place an item on a plinth* |

'I would like to put this bag down.' 'I will implinth it.'
'I would like to put this plinth down.' 'I will implinth it.'
'I would like to put this poem down.' 'I will implinth it.'

## ADDITIONAL INFORMATION

/ˈɪəʊː//ˈiːuː/

- 'They loaded me up with hape and pale pink lipstick.'
- 'I'll miss the dirty look he wpy gas, told me I had an abscess (eww), drilled out some decay and took $200 out of my pocke'ed O
- This selection of peep-toe boots, hpeared at first.'
- 'She wasn't even that pretty wiww" faxfords and stud of high school in my public school career and I've got to study for finals... eww!w'
- en on my feet (eww) sometimes.'ded short boots (I'm sorry, Ggets that particular beat... eww.'lue ey lemon. ewt.'ctor is higc6 more days
- She looks like a baked dancing then I feel like eww you're just staring at my boobs.'ape I have
- 'An "eww" from the children caused'They're funny because y brother.'th ssible sincher cont them to part and laugh.'men h of
- We wouldn't like to be the s see the ligh
- 'Big hair and pencil skirts (eww) ked me out bect?'the "e
- ctucci, but eww) should notlled Tanner ts, eww Kasha wannabould give you whday.' face aause at first I'ma what has been trampled into that carpet'ly makes her scarier when she turns on Christine.'
- 'Oh eww I just catreet clee yawned in your'I w
- 'eww, how can you eat thaner who  b'But that's also no'ew,n adding in, the ' eww... boys have cooties ' years.'t poigh-heel'It sinkyou went "eww!"'
- 'One glove was... eww... in the t
- w I'd hate to thih, but that on other wish I was as tough as the ski'Yeah, I'm eveith that disgusting old dog breath, and oilet, and theas filthy.'

are they one banana
nursing

one banana nursing
in a vase

but for the duct tape
for most of the night

we meet in the middle eat meat and middle

in arranging all the weather
all the weather in advance

are they one dried sun-dried tomato
warts and all

are they one arranging
one arranging two

## MY HEART LEAPS UP WHEN I BEHOLD
*After Enrst Jandl after Wordsworth*

May harsh hold sweet firm spigot bung tree yew tree icicle

He race gimlet    in into at inside lake waterfront

So thus so much this way so really which how much sees once provided may
    runs perpetration

So thus so much this way so really looks nigh near Emma scything

So thus so much this way so really oh such  territory   once provided   arse butt
    rumbles

Ear lug leaky to lick   with by at    including ovule

See steeply upright high-pitched smashing Norwegian sponsor [he loves
    racing journals] red scything

In at inside trendy dough batter Kurt smudge the bumph may all the more the
    beer wallop

Tree German German bayonet shearing clip alp nightmare animal eggs

## BIND US TOGETHER LORD

Not with a bulfinch or hawkmoth
bind us together with
little ropes, little ropes
with unforeseen consequences
beyond our young minds
unencumbered by primary care trusts
tufted vetch and larceny
unprepossessing circuitry
and judgemental attitudes glimpsed
in the shrubbery lies
loose tea; a selection of loose teas,
too loose for repetition in the knot garden.
Legerdemain. Slip of the tongue.
Pickpockets in light trousers.
Tomorrow the futures market. Today.
Pork bellies. Pork scratching in the compost.
Beef dripping from the eaves.
A non sequitur is the basket your head drops into.
Exactly. Sugar cube.
Toes. Dreaming spires.
In the marketplace for sequins. Fat sequence.
Five Harry Secombes. Three coins in a fountain.
Which one will the fountain bless?

PETROC TRELAWNY

*After Tim Atkins after Petrarch*

'll often talk an awful lot about tahini.
Roofed over and thatched with all these stems of orchids,
he judges a male's worthiness by the sounds he makes.

Rock-like clouds appear
to gather in the grasslands of Wyoming.
No wind & not much rain.

This is the moment he has been working towards:
he has decorated his parlour with deer dung and charcoal
but hasn't counted on all this sprouting fungus.

and so forth. Jack in the hedge hedges his bets and a doodle of sorts becomes an upper lip as you look in the mirror that is, in fact, a table on which I have placed a pattern like a feathered stone which might not sink if dropped into the nearest river, but float up and away into the evening air thick with midges whose wings are laden with incense. The midges rise and fall. Their wings beat the incense laden air so that it passes over our faces on the river bank and refreshes our expressions which were at risk of sliding down the river bank and falling into the water in a state of torpor. Or is it Torpenhow, pronounced Trepenner as in Trepanner or a Trapeze artist pronounced Tarpaulin but spelled backwards like a black ball rolling to our feet on a table on which is a mirror or a river or a doodle, of sorts, in which one thing becomes *on* which, becomes another *in* which until another becomes just another and that's a doodle becoming clear. Clear of soup and clear of purpose; a river purpose nosing carefully through the polluted waters of the Yangtse where the incensed reeds are smoking, lost in thought.

on Peckham Rye

with RB Kitaj

a halfpenny a year

from A.J. Ayer

# THE MAID OF BUTTERMERE

Buttermere is made of butter, mere butter,

but
the Buttermere maid is made of Buttermere butter, not mere butter. The Buttermere maid made the mere more merry, made beer for the mere, made the mere more beery. Barmaid Maud made the beer more beery more barmy, Maud made the mere mutter: ach mutter, meer mutter, das meer mutter, mère mutter, mère die mutter, mutter de la mer die mutter, mère mutter mère mutter, Walter de la Mare mutter, merde,

but
the mad maid of Buttermere made smears of Buttermere, made smears of smut on the smeary mere of Buttermere, the maid made me merry with the beer, but smutty, made me merry, made me smeary of the butter on the butt, made me smear me smeary Mary, made smeary Mary weary, Mary weary weary,

but
more butter made Maud mad, mad Maud made more, made more, made marmalade, more marmalade maid than beer or buttermaid, Maud made more. The marmalade maid laid in marmalade, ladled marmalade, laid down laws to ladle in marmalade. Marmalade marmalade, mermaid mad, marmalade Maud made the madder lake marmalade, made the mere more madder, made Crummock Water,

but
the maid of Buttermere smeared mere words, mere words, mere crumbs utter words, mere crumbs, but smears utter words, words utter crumbs, crumbs words, words crumbs, crumbs utter Crummock of the mere word water. Crummock Water ought to utter, ought to utter buttocks, but water butts ought to utter otters, buttock otters, buttock otters, otter buttocks, utter bollocks uttered backwards, butter no parsnips.

## RED SOCK IN YELLOW BOX

*After Robert Filiou and G.K. Chesterton*

I
A red sock in a yellow box

One can easily understand
A red sock in a yellow box


II
So that a man sitting in a chair
Might suddenly understand
That he was actually alive
And be happy

With
A red sock in a yellow box


III
One cannot put one's foot in the same river twice.
One cannot even put the same foot in the same river twice.
It's hard to explain why but one cannot. One has tried.

One can however fall in the same canal repeatedly

One can
One canal
One can easily

## SMOOTH AND BALD

In Peru, anyone who wishes to fly eats a light seed that floats with the wind.
My mother's favourite was the mashie niblick.

A game of quoits or figures of eight
using concentric circles of rope
above the washing line, clear above the marram grass, clear above the garden wall,
but there is no high purpose, no endgame.
No Papua New Guinea.

And the wheatfields of salty blueness
become conscious of being a reservoir of grace
all greasy as swivels in the egg factory
all talk of a walking cure using
a range of gently increasing slopes
to gradually heal the 'tired heart'.

What is good is light; whatever is divine moves on tender feet
according to Nietzsche.
Goosefat that's kind in gravy.
My Mother's favourite.

## FOR JACK

*For Jack Collom (8 November 1931 – 2 July 2017)*

Pieter Corneliszoon Plockhoy
also Pieter Cornelisz Plockhoy van Zierikzee
or Pieter Cornelius van Zurick-zee

also Riley Puckett the first man to sing about sauerkraut
or Bart Plantenga who put the yodel into ampersands:
&lt;em&gt;YodelinHi-Fi&it;em&gt;

also Trout Pomeroy
good to meet you Trout

also the DeZurik (or Cackle) Sisters
who 'left her standing there (with a doodad in her hair)'
or Alabama's Felt Twins, Gertrude and Gesna

or Gertrude and Gertrudes
Jekyll-Rose and Bell

also Abercrombie, Gertrude (1909–1977): 'I paint the way I do
because I'm just plain scared.
I mean, I think it's a scream that we're alive at all – don't you?'

# KINGFISHERS AND RELATED WORKS

To loosen each eye tooth I am myself again more recently with Gertrude unpacking her Gertrude. Chicken and potato in which and for which we have waited with a lamp of forgiveness as we meander through the woods past the Japanese Knotweed and only there, because I am a man of unclean lips, and I dwell in the middle of a people of unclean lips, do we look up and see water avens, look up in the dictionary and see the meaning of this discreet and most sophisticated flower of damp woodlands in which sadly still there is an absence of kingfishers for Hans Waanders. Een wandeling in het Neandertal, Duitsland. Bezoek aan pre-historische grot in Font de Gaume, Dordogne, Frankrijk. Twijgen (perches) om op te vissen in Vézère en Auvezère, Frankrijk. Publicatie van 'Kingfishers and related works', bronvermelding a sinuosity, or turning, esp. of a river; a maze, a transitive verb winds about in a circuitous course from a secret and parallel footpath between two hedges to nodding, drooping, cure-all, a watercolour indian chocolate and each one had six wings; with twain he covered his face, and with twain he covered his feet, and with twain he did fly.

# THE SITUATION OF POETRY
*After Ernst Jandl*

If I did not know everything has a beginning and an end I know that poetry often precedes suicide and always death. But it must not.

It is to do everything anywhere, the poems, and there are a total of many who do it, and anyone who does it, takes care of the others who do it, or he does not care about them. And anyone who does, takes care of the others, who do not, or he does not care about them. And so they ·write as one and the other like this and not at another, and so read the one way and the other like all the others are not. But they are all together now and a little praise and wailing will be both barely audible. This is not a conversation about poetry or poets. It must not.

This is not a conversation.

So much depends
upon

a Regency Whiplash Curve
Basket Capital

glazed with Raphaelesque
water lilies

beside the William and Mary style
Chinoiserie

## SWEET, FRUITY, FLORAL AND GRASSY (FOR FINN)

I am edging closer to the explicit use of euphemism
foraging in Crepis and Hebe flowers respectively
dominated by False Oatgrass and a distinct waist.
Even then the mothers pretend to be surprised
as the waters cover the sea parsnip soup belch
brightly coloured felt fishes part and parcel
of Thanks be to God try growing Candytuft
or Poached Egg plant sharp eyes like Coleridge
which is odd or even recognised as not to be too tidy
leaf litter used as a flagship but I've also been told
you don't get them in Worcestershire so what
could they be? We don't know. The toast is crisp. My son
is spreading, whistles a blend of honeys from around the world.

# AU SECOURS

An Earl in a red bush
A pearl in the ointment
A pig in clover

The mountain and the valley folds
The rabbit ear also
but an ear for what?

For reasonable adjustments
And no mistake

Let me explain:

'C'est monstrueux', says Eugène Ionesco,
using a rather nice walking stick to denounce
the whole of the London scene before him.

And not just London – he means everything.

The inscription on his tomb in Montparnasse cemetery reads:

Prier-le Je Ne Sais Qui
J'espère : Jesus-Christ.

Pray to the I don't-know-who:
Jesus Christ, I hope.

Meaning what and for whom?
For snowfall. That's fatal.
A heavy dew even.

We're all undone
in the long run
we all have to play cricket
and eat peaches
about the door
                    handles and windows
            falling off
                    whatever kind of guarantee
we might ever have had

## THREE-HOUR STINTS

Given crawfish, some personality and planks
the butchers whistle in the road
and cry into what theory she had left.

That same winter
in a Spanish basket
she called it the Bible
set aside two glass jars
of Kiki but Kiki had gone moonlight
woodwind and wild
strawberry tart tobacco tins.

## TO SHUT EVERY WINDOW WITH AN APPLE
## TREE (19 JUNE)

I have been a lucky man.
Bees frequent my chimneys.
Wood Strawberries begin to come.
Men shear their sheep.

Great Honeydew.
Barley in ear on the sands.
Crops of Cherlock
among the springcorn.

Thunder has come to settle
on my balm of Gilead Fir
as I lie under the trees
in a giant spoon

and the afternoon changes
from clear to cloudy
and back to clear again
like drops of water

in which, I believe,
you are slowly coming into view
holding a Cumberland sausage ring, some rosemary,
a frying pan and a chair leg

unconvincingly.

## OF SILESIA

the forests thrilling the most clearly
cough flowers and birch trees
at the same time winter in
seeing as is not what I see
I see the glass of red wine
but it was Sunday
and I said I'm going to cotton
packet sugar cube keen
said I'm keen to write that fact
all too fresh and the rotten
namely milk myself
in the hospital garden without
an outrage out an orange
of tongue and fern
the use of Ely gone
off the lawn that will be Monday's
before going back to bed
I hold back the urge

He who chooses to forgive, is forgiven, but
he who chews his loofer gives the wrong impression.

And that's all.
And that's all?
And that's all.

Well, thank you anyway.

'And doesn't that smell like ham and eggs?
No, that smells like *bacon* and eggs.
*Bacon* and eggs, *ham* and eggs, oh gee!
Mr Lindbergh made Paris.
But I made God's own heaven you see,
And there ain't no land like Dixieland to me.'

Trumpet solo.

SAIPPUAKAUPPIAS

An archaic soap-seller and palindrome I am going to have fish
for lunch swallowed up by the idle and groundless rumour of gorse
a place for keeping geese or a sloping relish for going about
staring like a fool in narrow passages between mountains mawkish
for sweet meat like circular plates three parts this to one part
crab apple with shelves for cups and plates and the like
and a single curvilinear boon companion composed of flattery
snarls abreast a buffer to the piston the point at which evil
or severe affliction prevents it giving way to eight o'clock's abrupt
hair played out on the ice's office of employment
or a curtain for scoops or scrapes in which or whereupon
has drains our sanity yellowed by soft words ushered
once in a while from house to house with a low peevish cry

## FUR COATS IN TAHITI
*Written through Yoko Ono's 'Snow Piece (Tape Piece III)'*

*Take a tape of the sound of the*   Tupperware   spectacled neatly; intelligent,
freely spoken but a little shy in chestnut-coloured corduroy   *snow falling*
started out as idle play but ends   with greater respect for royalty
We're in Bob's room   *This should be done in*   a matter of weeks? Yikes the chu:
in hammocks between the trees'   chewed face   burst water pipes
just one will do to get rid of it   *the evening*   ice cream tub
full of urine   mer-si-fool-i given to using mercury   in the Quaker lavatory
to listen   *Do not listen to*   shoe box   sunlight   token gesture   Spoonbill
We're in Bob's room in the margins   maritime enamel   *the tape*   sewn into
Delibes   parachutes   Edinburgh zoo   and one way or another so have I
with Russ Conway, Mrs Mills   a few rarities   monogamous and noisy
as Leicester cheese.   *Cut it and use it as string*   as they inflate their throat sacs
within range of the East Thames corridor   *to tie gifts with*   Pink Onions
Dry skinned reptiles have more options

## CHOOSE ANY ANIMAL IN THE PARK

The Siamang gets about the canopy of the forest by 'brachiation',
swinging from hand to hand. The baboon's ischial callosities are
highly developed, bright vermillion and… nice try but you really
need to work on your short words.

Maurice sounds like Sheila.
Mother sounds like Bach
as in German
as in get
as in my hat
but with the lips spread wide
sounds rather like quid at the beginning
of a huge   fat   summer   face down
my dress in the garden face down
is rather like choosing to choose
my pullover over
your gate &
blowing fantastic raspberries on her arms.

There are purple stripes in the Tiger.
There is a Rodrigues fruit bat or Zorro Volador the 'flying fox'.
This dragon has two heads.
Why aren't you writing anything down?

# LIMITED HEADROOM

Finding himself anew in the present Horace Walpole and the three Persian Princes
of Serendipity looked for one thing and found another.

Once you're up in the hay loft
kick the ladder away –

> The farmhouse is in the wing mirror
> tiny windows like cupboard doors.
> The wind is making something of it in the gorse bushes.
> The long midwinter shadow of the car on the road is like a tiered jelly
> and we are sitting in small cells of light near the top.

Passing cars are disparaging.

Then she took him back to earth and turned him into a grasshopper.
And lo it came to pass
the kidneys Cleopatra
chose the jaw
dewdrops clinging to I have nothing to say
and I am saying it
I have nothing to do and I am doing it
I have nothing to wear and I am wearing it

The American sea is all I can hear
How do you do that?
I'm sure you do once you see it
and so on and so forth with the lips of a deer

And lately a newt
in fact
all three species of newt

Seeking only to pander to a fad
is it worth mentioning tennis elbow?
Athlete's foot?
Achilles heel?
How about my nascent piles?

     The very act of opening the wings
     to reveal the interior

               the duck-like belly is burst open
               the night sky is lit up with tiny fires

     There is limited headroom in this underpass
     and so we, the elated, need to exercise little caution.

A shoe factory in Cockermouth for the elderly
Late again with rhubarb in February February March
The alchemists and rope makers live in the long alleyways
beneath the castle and brewery which lead down to the riverside.

One reluctantly agrees to have his balls felt to see how real they are

Later on in primary school I am trying to juggle satsumas.

On Hansel and Gretel's first birthday in the woods
there is the sweet smell of success in the green grocer's
a sweet smell of blood in the butcher's
and in the optician's the smell of lenses
coming gradually into focus in the early morning citrus
of a backroom overlooking the musical river

The enigma of content triumphs in the flying fishes
Our gaze wanders from motif to motif
to more teeth in a glass cylinder with an ebony base-cum-upturned hurdy gurdy

     A huge blue finely veiled globe rises from the water
     An uneaten apple in her left hand fondles her partner's genitals
     There is a clearing
     There are no children in this paradise
     only life-like songbirds and ducks on which tiny people are
     eating fruit the size of an armchair
     while another has his buttocks towards her
     in a state of permanent 'becoming'
     that blurs the boundary between them

This is where we all come from sitting on the goldfinch – the young man looks like
he's listening to his personal stereo smiling to himself, being fed, open beaked, in
their nest
     through the back door as it were

The vet's waiting room. A throng of people and the pleasure pool. Biomorphic
protuberances come into play squeaming through molluscs into strawberries
between ankles and trunks and rubbing oneself upon them in a glass cylinder full
of silage in the blue gone awry that stops her juggling

Why wouldn't you want to make one of those latest examples of a mandrake in a
coffin come from Lubeck? What happens on Sunday? Ludovic Kennedy?

The Bereavement Sisters long gone arrear
suggest that we are   if you will       as it were   what exactly?

dealing with miniature coffins
drinking copious cups of tea
in order to feel the jouissance of a full bladder frequently emptied

and entered a hypnotic trance while doing so
The Dream of the Urinals, yes?

The man behind the counter quips 'Are you pregnant?'
He has so many meat pies on his tray.
Sliding along feels nice but I'm nervous holding the baby.
We have a large dog to look after now. A Great Dane.
Yes, you have a great day. *Hic Rhodus Hic Salta.* Engels
Somehow slipshod and dreary. *Here is Rhodes/the rose. Jump/dance* hic *here.*

I'm eating the meat pies despite a presence behind me
that makes me think of the outhouse at Allonby.
You stoop to get down to get through the doorway – which has no door
and enter the room – which has no roof.
What would you keep in here apart from rain?

This time we are leaving Ethiopia at the airport.
Marita is caught with a sewing kit in her luggage and fined £60. I knew this
    would happen.
Not for the first time we are pouring money down the drain.
There is some confusion over roads
causing you to lose your place.

We wade out into icy seas to launch a loaf of bread to celebrate the birth of
    a baby
Or vice versa

Look, that hole in the carpet is also a hole in my arse
Look, look.
Oh, oh.
Oh, look.

Tip to tiptoe goes the careful lodger
boulders rolling down the hill after Buster
and the hundreds of brides-to-be.

The little boxes are of wood as a result of which we were left
rough shaped and each is covered with a flat lid secured by wire or brass nails
and teeth.
No, not teeth, no teeth from adolescence onwards.
Words. Lourdes. My dentist. Keith. Leith docks, a history of
the door is always too small.

One is in this context inclined to forget that in any given time few ideas of
hope and fear survive. In july 1836 some children playing on the North eastern
side of Arthur's seat came across a peculiar collection of objects. Tea cups in
an auditorium. Patterns everywhere on the floor on the walls and ceilings like
this: eyelashes up and eyelashes down. Hummingbirds mean something
in teak oil.

        lighting in the alcove – hot feet full of shoes
as the children nibble at the house
the coy red walls
framed hair loops from Queen Victoria
or an ox from the feast

And lately a newt
in fact all three species of newt

But a lack of chairs, a distinct
lack of chairs
Laissez-faire. Throw it away. I *have* thrown it away.

It feels like the right time to leave Ethiopia, this time [for London]
    Ch34 the Afar Graves
    Ch 35 J&M in hotel room. They talk
    Ch36 Sex

I have *not* thrown it all away
An apple after all tastes like idiocy
[1. under the kitchen table
2. behind the Buddha
3. in the woodstove]

Anywhere we want we will hear the music played.
Every horse is capable of swimming.
Look at a dewdrop. You'll see everything in it. Go on. Give it a try. Give it a try.

I soak my socks in the green splotch
to balance the red splotch that vanilla can give.

On a mat appears
onomatopoeia's
a sloth with a swelling
in the pit of his stomach

The red dream house
for the elderly is all thick residential carpets
dark chocolate, beetroot and pear
or dark chocolate, pear and hair
but no teeth either way (see above).

* * *

THE PENCIL METHOD

'Lying in bed would
be an altogether
perfect and supreme
experience if only
one had a colored
pencil long enough
to draw on the ceiling.'

Lying on the ceiling
would also be altogether
if only one only
had a pencil long enough
to draw on experience.

A pencil long enough
to draw altogether
in bed on the ceiling.

*


On Lying in Bed
by
G.K. Chesterton

By Lying in Bed
on
G.K. Chesterton

In Lying on Bed
On buying in lead

in Chesterfield

gawp
gawp at
gawp in at

gawp at in
gawp in at gawp at in
gawp at in        gawp at in        gawp at in

gawp in at
at in at
gawp in at        at in at

gawp at
in at in at
gawp at   in at in at

in at in
in
in at in at

in gawp at        in gawp at in

at gawp
in
at gawp

gawp in
at
gawp in

gawp in
gawp at

```
gawp in at          gawp at

gawp in at          gawp at in
gawp in at          gawp at in
gawp in at          gawp at in
```

Clement Attlee
MP

while his mind
is otherwise engaged

playing the tuba

*

About my playing the tuba.
Seems like a lot of fuss
has been made about that.

Everybody does something silly
when they're thinking

*

the Labrador and Poodle
are derived from do little

*

tuba players running around loose. I can't begin to tell you
how sick of it he was running around

loose tuba

*

this revived my writerly enthusiasm
such that I now have
mastered the art of being patient
with the aid of my pencil

*

the unique bliss of the pencil method
the noblesse oblige of tensile steel
the bleak abbess of the penal colony
you need less of this

less of the nibbles
urethra

or una
on the buses
with Una and the pencil stubs

the purposeful, uninterrupted, yet dreamy
hand movements
of Una Stubbs the Newquay by-pass
Newquay Newbury
Thank you Matt the Matt Stubbs by-pass

the you and each bleak clique
less the blue neeps blissed out
kissed in bleaberry

then each creak's blessing
of the unskilled Methodist
parsnips in the distillery

you need the poplar the poplar
you need to piss off the poplar
not the yew tree

you need less than all of this
you need less of the pencil method
and more of the birth pangs

        *


by means
of the pencil

by means of the pencil
I slowly
freed myself

by means of
slowly
I freed myself laboriously


from the *Observer Book of Dogs*

        *


writing remains
the non-human remains
pressed up against
seldom blasé

        *

It calms me down and cheers me up

\*

For some it's a
a tree trunk: it's a
straining to assert
a tree trunk: it's a
a tree trunk: it's a
a tree trunk: it's a
long trudge to Spain
glued together to
ecstasy. What is
a tree trunk: it's a
brass rubbing from a
double decker bus
the dozen or more
ten years
glued together to
children adding
this reservoir, she
blue sheets, upon
this reservoir, she
blue sheets, upon
fresh marks over old
associations
these bears the title
the books turn into
fresh marks over old
these bears the title
rambles, bemused
be grasped if only
the book turns into
brickwork along

rambles, bemused
that such
dripping pens
on a rail journey
in the doldrums
that such indeed
apprentice clerk
rambles bemused
proves the pen
and potato method
Hallelujah Mesopotamia
the need he seems
he seems to need
to carry telescopes

*

once wriggling free
I learned again, like a little boy
bilingualism, and
tangled plant life
which is nowadays
the source of
the scratching and
another need to

*

kilometre-long
giddy and
sources unrolls
quickly like
linguine or a
need to set limits

and indeed seems to
unroll quickly like
our hours arrghse
at a stretch
which are filled in
to rough quilting or
feel she is sewing
annotations which
need to set tinnitus
to rough quilting or
wavering between
normal reading as in
daydream tedium
replacing
her early days
should shed
should remove from

\*

a box. Many of these
collected. One of
various

\*

teaching jobs

\*

turret-like, a tiny
challenge in
the skyline,
crabbed, yet we

desire for clarity
a child at school, she
recalls the quiet
of letters: she
may have something
which has cropped
the scratching and
"It was magical
upon the lofty
and freedom. I was
wobbling and
scarcely anywhere
up in a corner
upon the lofty
off-cuts of timber
Geneviève
made her think of


\*


the worm-eaten
part of the afternoon


\*


starts with an
haphazard and
diligent yet apparent
incompleteness


\*


haphazard and
woozily oblong

*

feeling". It's a bit as
as if there were a
Burton-on-Trent in
dépaysement, a term
she repeatedly took
repeatedly by harks
the case with the
things in is another

*

a real breakdown
in my hand
a sort of cramp
from whose clutches
I freed myself by
scudding across the
sensation of her nib
and Carlo Zinnelli. I
announce the
smudged peaks
at the outer limits of
even lying next to it,
the apparent
straining these
surfaces and a
major reference to the
tiny oasis in a desert
she has dubbed her
*Dictionnaire Illustré*

*

with other rooftop perches

*

uncles, aunts, cousins.
or the ends of logs.

*

the state of kelp
helps
to staple the hen

*

dark and fearsome
in their glaring
anatomies
paste and loose
first rode through
the revelation of an
album of
children adding loves
making stamping
letters. My body is
content
Berberat, August
content
wooden outhouse
an ascetic cell. What
influences, rules
on white paper. A
box. Many of these

*

But *in toto*
does that mean
anything?

*

I mean

I mean
what do people do all day

what do people do
all day

all day what do
people do all day

what do people
do all day

what doop
eeple do
all day

what doop
eeple doop

eeple doople
day

what deeple doo whap

I mean
what?

KENNETH KOCH UNCORKED

O

O

O

O

O

O

O

O

O

O

O

O

O

O

O

O

O

O  O

O

O

O

O

O

O

O

O

O

O

O

O

O

O

O

O

O

O

\* \* \*

## THE ORDERLY WORLD

*for Jan*

**axolotl** (ak'-sō-lotl) *n.* [Mex.]
a tailed amphibian found in Mexico

albeit Albert in a palace pertaining to, or produced
by a short eared mastiff skillet in nickel extracts
gutta-percha by boiling in alcohol in
alarming manner in a boiler inability
to speak in the softer part of the wood
next to the bark, the embryo and skin
of many seeds or a deficiency in water related
to one of the varieties of fret ornament
and a peculiarity in the eyes
of the softer part of the book
in which visitors enter their names:
Resinous compound
Cheerful readiness
G. *ouron*, urine
Embargo
a contrivance for awakening persons from sleep to the bleak,
a silvery white fish skilled in alchemy, nickel, copper and zinc

**bungle** (bung'-gl) *v.t.* [Sw. *bangla*] to make
or mend clumsily ; to manage awkwardly ; – *v.i.*
to act clumsily ; – *n.* a clumsy performance; a gross
blunder

To be pungent by degrees supporting windlasses twice and twisted
as tennis for unglazed porcelain acrid croquet leap year one piece
of the pieces makes a sound like saltwork sarcasm a dark brown
colour at the end of the pipe through which a bird lays eggs
in China lacking the faculty of concentration to let in a light
mouthful or large frog a clumsy boat fine kind of lawn a wide
sleeved nightingale of the Persian as in onion whose occupation
it is to build the buttocks one half of which the hydrogen is the
quality of being bumptious or bulky a glass filled to the brim at a
theatre by the end of the pipe through which you unload cargo as
horse cheeks and throat of a crimson colour advocates the use of
an exclusively metallic currency of flour sugar eggs and marmalade
that has undergone a wild kind of organ used in teaching small
birds to sing a thick knob left on a sheet of plate-glass plum by
the end of the pipe through which it was blown to form separate
compartments in the porcelain nightingales of the Persians

**curliness** (kur'-li'-nes) *n.* state
of being curly.

The contours of a cup
but no blood is abstracted
from coniferous trees and the like.

Snarling with orange peel
paralyses the motor neurons and causes
the incumbent to restrain a fruit-weevil.

A house in which sugar is drained is dried
for the ringing of a bell at nightfall.

A ringlet of hair played on ice or eight o'clock.
A disease of peach trees tending to curl / a churl.

A small kind of grape
is in circulation.

**divergence** (di-ver'-jens) *n.* a
receding from each other in radiating
lines; a going further apart.

An advocate of disunion digs ditches.
A good one and an evil one who both believe
in the broad-leaved Pepperwort
which has been said to fall asunder
in praise of wine, also to plunge
into water, or the unconscious repetition of words,
headfirst from more than one direction.

**Egyptologist** (e-jip-tol'-ō-jist) *n.*  a student
skilled in the antiquities and hieroglyphics of Egypt.

One that goes out feathery
to bring about peace in short sentences.

And the eighteenth part of anything
ejects or dispossesses another of his land.

Vegetables in the Arctic regions are an expression
of slight surprise as a species of clumsy antelope
of greasy lustre slips by, testing the density of olive-oil
and readily returns to its previous state
after being overtaxed.

**frutescent** (fróò-tes'-ent)  *a.*
[*L. frutex*, shrub] becoming shrubby ;
shrubby.

fub, fubby, plump, chubby
as doubtful as wood
Leonard Fuchs the botanist
Johann N Fuchs the chemist

barren ; ineffectual ; vain ; a swarm
of little people coloured green
as meat heated in lard is coloured green
by the presence of chromium

an abscess in the ear
the frog of a horse's foot
is made of wheat is made
foolish or disordered by milk
balk to thwart with currant brings
to nothing one prolifically

**goetic** (gō-et'-ik) *a.*
of, or relating to goety

a marbled green doctrine
cobwebs from blade to blade
the opera-glass fragility of its tail

that which is song; a catch from the valley
yellow substance foot high
pods a soft talk teal

**heroship** (hē′rō-ship) *n.*
the state of being a hero

a tax on salt
dry spear
Cadiz

a cockeyed idle
meaning triangular
to a native or inhabitant of pregnancy
and the Manx pectoral makes for
a language of extended pouch

my sweetheart   menial   squint-eyed   zodiac
is binding the others in severity to a dwelling-house

**incalculable** (in-kal'-kū-la-bl) *a.*
[L. *in*, not and E. *calculable*] not capable of
being calculated ; beyond calculation ; very
great.

An unlucky space evil ovoid
with whom one is in love

at right angles


Without reckoning on
setting fire to the Spaniards

the rules of art
want nutrition

**job** (job) *n.* [O.F. *gob*, a mouthful, *c.f. gobble*]
a piece of work; chance work; labour undertaken
at a stated price, or paid for by the hour or day;
a lucrative business or transaction.


a basket-work palanquin
slung from a pole

peculiar, or pertaining
to charcoal contiguity

same as jostle
close together

coarse and fairly
carpet

**Kantian** (kan'-ti-an) *a.* of,
or belonging to, the German philosopher,
Immanuel Kant, 1724–1804, or his school
of philosophy.

A Calcutta
kind of rough
retching warp

Back down
keep in and
keep under

A token of friendship
repaired for the wanton
made of seal skins
and a tub for a ship
and the binding

**lardaceous** (lar-dā-sgus) *a.*
consisting of, or resembling, lard.


Larry see Lorry the loose
bacon beetles it flowers and

placed above a door
bling a lion

only two
bling a
link

with a fork at one end

**merdivorous** (mer-div'-u-rus) *a.* [L.
*merda*, dung, and *vorare*, devour] feeding on dung.

a harbinger
by metamorphism
*pl.* the knees the best parts
of iron tool tapering
to the point of marriage

hand to hand combat
in the bowls of tobacco pipes
with spongy pith passages
of stark pigmeat

**nodical** (nod-i-kal) *a.* relating to the node

From the letters of one's name
to the origins of life
in sexless short-staple woollens.

An elastic plurality given to nombles to numbles
depends on a wall of scantling outcries.

The risen Christ plants several,
combed out from the long aversion,

as an eating ulcer on the face
wanders about in search of pasture.

**oversman** (ō'-verz-man) *n.* an
overseer; an umpire

to strike the toe of the hind foot
is to sleep too long

to grow beyond the fit
is to rate too high

to hear more than was intended
is to becloud

to do too much
is too great a dose

to wear one shoe worn over another
worn over and over     over another

is to overjoy the umpire

**Pullman-car** (pool'-man-kar) *n.*
[ *Pullman*, American inventor] a railway sleeping
or palace car.

a scarf and hat
small bones
stop plumage

one that vomits
stuffing mattress
swallows in the dust

one is drawn towards
one's fallopians

pillowy and pad-like
throbbing in the sermons

**quaint** (kwānt) *a.* [L. *cognitus*, known] characterized by ingenuity or art; subtle; artificially elegant ; odd and antique ; curious and fanciful ; whimsical ; singular.

peat-bog quack a furnish fourth

by unit or units but sometimes of silver

**reinforce** (rē-in-fōrs) *v.t.* to strengthen
with new force, assistance, or support ; *esp.* to
strengthen, as an army or a fort with additional
troops, or a navy with additional ships ;— *n.* part
of a gun near the breech, which is stronger than
the rest of the piece.

abode ; retreat ; seclusion ;
privacy of the eye thereby
silent and taciturn

take back what has been said
unsaid defects hinder tracing
or toss back again

to one whose profession
was to produce a red colour
at the tip of the strop

**smokable** (smō'-kạ-bl) *a.* capable
of being smoked.

smutch
or obs-
at; to for
like, or as
with ink
not perf-
from ob-
blot; a
missive; to
such as
a blouse
cigar or pipe

The upper part laundry
of which the lines
or kindness
from a honeycomb
is the only part that turns to meet the wind

**tush** (tush) *int*. pshaw ! (an exclamation
indicating check, rebuke, or contempt).

a want of relish rubs with turpentine
green and blue of the eastern continent
turns a spit spiral
post or pin
green soup
turns up
one half equipage
one hence manoeuvre
a beam full tollgate take
punctures trifling
so idle talk spins by the architecture
so called stitch peculiar
like the greek letter naked

**umlaut** (óòm'-lout) *n.* [Ger} name given by Grimm to the vowel-change in one syllable, through the influence of one of the vowels *a, i,* or *u* in the syllable that comes next.

an ochreous navel string
one of the vowels
above the hinge

one syllable
per
hernia
of the larger kind
bearing umbels
to the rays of the sun

an appendage
not unpleasing
not accommodated
not acquitted
not forgiven
not even
insured

**velouté** (vē-lóò'-tā) *n.* [F.} velouté –
sauce, a white sauce made by boiling down
veal, poultry, and ham.

an artificial language
made by a horse going sideways
round a contrivance with glass
taps as if a tenor be lower green than red
and live in peace and quietness at home
in dresses and trims and
what is thus laid on
wholly in two rhymes
disguises with a thin leaf
a superior kind of reverence
which do not weave nest
so hung as to having
a good long nap

**whopper** (hwop'-er) *n*. one that whops; a monstrous lie

in consequence of which
teeth in wheels
with difficulty and noise
contemptuous
in making cheese so as
to submerge in particular
on which ; on what
of which ; of what

a round piece of wood in any case
resembles as with a hawk's wing
a minor complaint
to a Scotch Presbyterian
going from house to house
with a turnpike sailor
to make a living singing
puff of air

**X, x,** the twenty-fourth letter of the English alphabet, is a superfluous letter.

**yawn** (yawn) *v.i.* [A.S. *geonian*] to open
the mouth involuntarily through drowsiness,
dulness, or fatigue; to gape; to open wide; to
be eager; – *n.* involuntary opening of the mouth
from drowsiness; a gaping; an opening wide.

366 days to three feet bark yelp
yes Mandarin; yes any; indeed;
Chinese shrieking woodpecker
spun from natural fibres
tuber esculent to boorish gaping

for eagerly as eagerly for goat is for African
raspberry much peat tells story
of which rope is composed
and neighbouring countries
at-a-gan out by straight course

**zuffolo** (zóò'-fõ-lõ) *n.* [It.] a small flute.
Also Zufolo.

whether suffering from or well versed in,
used as, taught by, having the character of,
carried on the back or scraped from the sides of,

or produced by some morbific principle that acts on the system
and spreads around the body like a girdle
alternately, with
and without syncopation

like zif or like zarf,
like zambomba
like zimbi like zoppo,
like zebub like zebub
like zobo zel zobo
like zein

# &

'Ampersand *n*. the sign &, meaning "and." 1835, formed in English by alteration of *and per se (=) and*, a phrase formerly found in glossaries, meaning "&" by itself = "and". From the Latin *per se*, meaning "by itself".'

But what use is & *by itself* in between nothing & more nothing with no possibility of being among others, in a crowd, *on* in + *gemang, gemong,* or
of being amorphous or amphibious as in Sir Thomas Browne, or
of popping some amphetamines and running amok [see AMUCK] with a unit of electric current adopted by the Paris Electric Conference of 1881?

I am just a small, bald figure sitting in an empty land offering you nothing from my upturned hand.

ACKNOWLEDGEMENTS

Grateful acknowledgements are made to the editors of the following publications in which some of the poems or versions of them first appeared: *The Best British Poetry 2015* edited by Emily Berry, (Salt, 2015), *Decals of Desire, Eleksographia, Magma, PN Review, Shadow Train, Like Starlings, The Clearing*.

I am also grateful to the Arts and Humanities Research Council and Midlands3Cities Doctoral Training Practice for funding research, part of which involved writing some of these poems.

Many thanks for those who helped in other ways with this book, especially Luke Kennard, Adrian Mallen, Marita Over, Ian Seed and Matthew Welton.

'H.C. Kind Man' and 'The Situation of Poetry' were derived initially from on line translations of texts by H.C. Artmann and Ernst Jandl.

'The Fine Art of Writing' is a variation on a sentence from Ernst Jandl's essay 'Technical aspects of composing poems' from *Die schöne Kunst des Schreibens* (*The Fine Art of Writing*).

'My Forthcoming Tomette' and 'Additional Information' are pieces of flarf which include text from the Collins online French—English dictionary.

'My heart leaps up when I behold' is a largely semo-definitional treatment of a literal translation back into English of Ernst Jandl's homophonic or 'surface' translation of Wordsworth's poem into German.

'Notes on *UM*' applies Tom Phillips's erasure procedure to his own 'Notes on A Humument'.

'So much depends' applies the Oulipian N+7 procedure to William Carlos Williams's 'So much depends' using *The Dictionary of Ornament* by Philippa Lewis (Pub Cameron Books, 1990).

'May in April' contains lyrics from Bix Beiderbecke's 'There Ain't No Land Like Dixieland To Me' and ends with his trumpet solo.

'The Pencil Method' includes text from G.K. Chesterton's essay 'On Lying in Bed'; Robert Walser's comments on the 'Pencil Method' he used in his 'microscripts'; Roger Cardinals' essay 'Geneviève Seillé: Beyond Reading' about the work of the outsider artist Geneviève Seillé; Len Lye's writing about doodling; the film 'Mr Deeds Goes to Town' and Richard Scarry's 'What Do People Do All Day?'

'Kenneth Koch Uncorked' is an erasure of the first ten pages of Kenneth Koch's *When the Sun Tries to Go On*, leaving just the exclamatory 'O's.

'The Orderly World' contains illustrations, near adjacent definitions and collaged text from A.M. Williams's *The King's English Dictionary* (British Books, 1933).